100 Creative Writing Activities

To Promote Positive Thinking

Karen Holford

*To Bernie, Bethany, Nathan and Joel
in appreciation of all the fun we've had
playing with words together.*

Contents

Preface

As soon as I learned to write I fell in love with words. As a child I made lists of rhyming words so I had a good supply for the funny little poems I wrote. As a teenager my grandfather taught me how to do cryptic crosswords and words inspired flexible creativity and mental gymnastics. Making up amusing anagrams, playing word games and writing stories meant I was never bored. The words in my head accompanied me and kept me entertained wherever I went, especially if I had a notebook and pencil in my bag.

As an adult I studied systemic psychotherapy to become a family therapist. I learned about narrative therapy and the power of words to change relationships and even people's lives. Looking at a story from a fresh perspective, and describing it with different words, could transform a person's world. I still find this work inspiring and exciting. I also learned the importance of asking questions that brought forth stories of people's strengths, hopes, joys and loves.

Over the years I wrote journal entries, jotted down ideas, listed things I was thankful for, researched my projects, wrote stories and articles, and put my dreams, prayers and hopes into words. Throughout the writing process I noticed that my ideas would form, change shape, develop and take me to new places. Sometimes I didn't know what I thought until I read my words on paper, and when I did, I could reflect on them, see the flaws, and refine them.

Recently, while working on a project with the Playfield Institute in Fife, I was introduced to Barbara Fredrickson's positive psychology research (Fredrickson, 2009). My experiences with the creative, hopeful and healing power of words were woven together with her discoveries about how to help people flourish by encouraging them to think about happy, fun, thankful, awesome, loving, interesting, inspiring and hopeful things.

Many of the people I worked with were reluctant to put pen to paper. They were afraid of writing the wrong things, misspelling words, or being judged, criticised and misunderstood. So I wanted to create some activities that would invite people to write about enjoyable things, and help them to focus on a wide range of positive experiences and thoughts. I also wanted to help busy professionals find attractive and easy-to-use activities to help their students and clients write in all kinds of fun, engaging and simple ways.

And so this project was conceived from a collection of ideas scribbled on a piece of scrap paper during a very long train journey. The ideas were shaped into sentences, the illustrations were imagined onto the page, and the manuscript was born. Speechmark's skilful staff have created this book. And now it's up to you – to take these pages and make them your own, in any way you like, exploring, creating, discovering, playing and sharing as you travel on a flourishing journey into your own positive thoughts.

Enjoy your writing!

Karen Holford, MA, MSc, DipCOT

> *No writing is a waste of time – no creative work where the feelings, the imagination, the intelligence must work. With every sentence you write, you have learned something. It has done you good.*
>
> *(Ueland, 1938, p19)*

Acknowledgements

Thank you to Dr Barbara Fredrickson for the special inspiration I received for this project after reading her book *Positivity* (Fredrickson, 2009).

Thank you to Dr Wendy Simpson at the Playfield Institute, Fife, for introducing me to Barbara's ideas about positive psychology. She encouraged me to develop creative ways to help families and young people explore positive thoughts, perspectives, experiences and ideas. I have really appreciated the Playfield Institute's very practical website at **www.handsonscotland.co.uk.**

Thank you to all the staff at Speechmark who enabled this book to come into print, especially Hilary Whates, Publishing and Product Development Manager.

Thank you to everyone who has encouraged me to enjoy all kinds of writing all through my life. Special thanks to my parents, Kate and Tony Welch, my aunt, Mary Barber, David Marshall, and my husband, Bernie.

Thank you to everyone who inspired me to think positive and uplifting thoughts throughout my life, especially during the challenging times.

And to the unknown lady who, over a century ago, chose the following Bible verse and painted it on the wall in my school hall, where I spent many hours thinking about it:

> *Whatever is true, whatever is noble, whatever is right, whatever is pure, whatever is lovely, whatever is admirable - if anything is excellent or praiseworthy - think about such things.*

(St Paul's letter to the Philippians, 4:8, Holy Bible)

How to use this book

This is a book full of ready-to-use creative writing activity pages. They are designed to stimulate writing by providing interesting and attractive projects. They are mostly quick and fun to do in order to help overcome the fear that some people have about writing lengthy prose.

The activities are presented in 10 sections, each promoting a different aspect of positive thinking. At the end of each section there is a list of writing activities in other sections in the book that may also encourage similar aspects of positive thinking.

This book may be used in many different ways: writers can write straight into the book; work on rough paper first and then write their final copy in the book; print the pages from the CD that accompanies this book or photocopy them to write on and store their work in a binder.

About the activities

The activities are designed to help the writer explore positive emotional experiences that may contribute to their well-being and mental health. They are not intended to explore painful emotional experiences that may open up more than the group leader or individual user can safely manage. The activities are designed to be simple, attractive and fun and they explore a wide variety of everyday writing styles and skills. The illustrations may help to inspire the writer and make their finished work look more attractive. The finished pages can be collected into personal folders or displayed on the wall.

Before you start to use an activity:

- It may be useful to try an activity for yourself first, so that you can understand how it works and be prepared to answer any questions, or so that you can show an example of your work.

- Think carefully about your client group and how they will experience the activity. The more familiar you are with your group, the easier it will be to choose suitable writing activities for their interests and abilities.

Speechmark

- If you are working in a group setting it is useful to 'warm up' the group with a related discussion before focusing on the writing activity, so that they are already playing with the ideas and concepts they will experience in the task.

- You may want to offer a choice of similar activities, or one activity that focuses on what you would like your client or student to explore.

After you have finished an activity it may be useful to keep records of how you used these activities, for example:
- when you used it
- who you used it with
- how you introduced the activity
- what went well
- any unexpected outcomes or challenges
- how you might adapt it for future use.

Using the material in your context

The following ideas are just suggestions to help you think of different ways you could use the material in your personal or work context.

Individuals can use the activities:
- to experiment with different kinds of creative writing in quick and easy projects
- to write on attractive pages that enhance the appearance of their writing and inspire their creativity
- to write something that may only take a few moments.

Teachers can use the writing projects in different ways with their students:
- to supplement class work
- to provide interesting homework tasks
- to encourage reflective thinking
- to create interesting classroom displays
- to stimulate thoughtful discussion
- to engage students socially in group activities
- to stimulate positive thinking in students, such as hopefulness, inspiration and gratitude
- to provide 'just for fun' activities as rewards for completing other class tasks

• to encourage reluctant writers to write by offering attractive and interesting projects that do not demand lengthy prose.

Speech and language therapists can choose a wide variety of tasks to suit older children and adults. They can use the writing projects in the book to:
• provide interesting writing tasks and homework
• stimulate group discussion
• encourage the development of handwriting skills
• encourage reflective and creative thinking
• provide sequencing and organisational tasks
• practise completing forms using interesting activities
• encourage clients to read and follow unusual instructions
• develop healthy and positive thinking skills
• provide amusing and fun activities that have a therapeutic purpose
• provide larger spaces for writing by enlarging the pages on a photocopier.

Psychologists may use the book in a variety of settings to:
• help clients focus on positive thinking skills and patterns
• nurture hopefulness
• encourage clients to think of others and be less focused on themselves and their concerns
• provide interesting group activities to build social skills.

Occupational therapists could use the material in the book to:
• provide practice for writing and fine motor skills (the pages also provide colouring activities if appropriate)
• develop social skills
• nurture positive and healthy thinking
• encourage sequential thinking.

Writing groups and libraries could use the book to:
• stimulate creative ideas that could be developed into other projects
• provide quick warm-up exercises
• encourage group interaction by using some of the activities that can be adapted for group use
• provide short writing projects so that everyone in a group has time to share their work.

Family therapists and other agencies working with families can use these activities to:

- provide quick and ready-to-use activities that can engage families with older children
- help the family focus on positive experiences together
- provide interesting family homework activities
- nurture hopefulness
- encourage family interaction
- help the family have fun together

The materials could also be useful in other contexts such as prisons, day centres, libraries, women's refuges, youth clubs and families.

Just for fun!

Laughter expresses our enjoyment of life and appropriate humour helps us to socialise and connect with those around us. Fun and playfulness are also important ways to maintain a positive emotional balance (Fredrickson, 2009). Various research articles suggest that laughter may also be an important aspect of healing, general well-being and social interaction (Provine, 2001), especially when the laughter is about non-dangerous situations, and is not at another person's expense.

The following writing activities are just for pure amusement, either for individuals or for use in a group. But they'll probably be most fun if they can be shared!

The funniest thing!

Write a short story about one of the funniest things that ever happened to you. If possible, write it as a script for a stand-up comedian.

Smile file

What makes you smile or laugh? Describe one thing that makes you grin or giggle in each of the smiley faces below.

Comedy critic

Write a review for one of the funniest films or shows you've ever seen. Write it so that the reader will really want to watch it too.

THE DAILY NEWS

www.dailynews.co.uk   **THE WORLDS FAVOURITE NEWSPAPER**   since 1867

FILM REVIEW

FILM OF THE YEAR

TITLE
DIRECTOR
CAMERA
DATE   SCENE   TAKE

Rhyme time

Write a funny limerick or rhyming poem about yourself.

There once was a writer from Rome,

Who decided to make up a poem. He wrote a few lines,

About porcupine spines

And then read them aloud to his gnome

The same letter story

Write a story where at least 8 out of every 10 words begin with the same letter. For example, 'Fearless Fred found four furry felines feeding frantically on fried fish…' How long can you make it? If you're in a group, play this together taking it in turns to add a fresh word to the story and being 'out' if you take too long to think of one!

A B C D E F G H I
B · · · · · · · · J
C · · · · · · · · K
D · · · · · · · · L
E · · · · · · · · M
F · · · · · · · · Z
G · · · · · · · · Y
H · · · · · · · · X
I · · · · · · · · W
J · · · · · · · · V
K · · · · · · · · U
L M N O P Q R S T

Giddy thoughts

Make a spiral of the words that just pop into your head! The catch is that each word you write in the spiral below must start with the last letter of the previous word. For example, a list of animals might read 'Elephantigerabbitortoisemunicornewt'.

Do you see any connections between your words? If you're doing this in a group, swap spirals at the end and see if you can read out each other's lists without getting giddy!

Flipside story

Write a familiar fairy tale from the perspective of one of the minor characters in the story or an unmentioned relative of one of the characters, such as a father. For example, Cinderella's dad (where was he when she was being used like a slave?), the fairy godmother (she seems to have a strange affection for rats and mice), Hansel and Gretel's dad (why was he such an irresponsible parent?). Be as creative and as funny as you like, and allow your character to tell their flipside story of a traditional tale.

The reverse alphabet story

Write a story where each word begins with a different letter of the alphabet, starting with Z. Each of the following words in the story must start with the previous letter of the alphabet, Z, Y, eX, W, V, and so on. For example, 'Zack Yelled eXcitedly, "Which Vehicle Undertook Tim's Snazzy Roadster?"'.

Z
Y
X
W
V
U
T
S
R
Q
P
O
N
M
L
K
J
I
H
G
F
E
D
C
B
A

Wordsearch

Create a wordsearch puzzle of at least 20 positive adjectives you'd use to describe yourself. Write a list of the words you want to include in the puzzle. Then fit them into the grid below. Your words can run horizontally, vertically and diagonally, backwards or forwards. Make a copy and give it to a friend to solve. (Tip: use a pencil with an eraser – you may need to make a few changes along the way.)

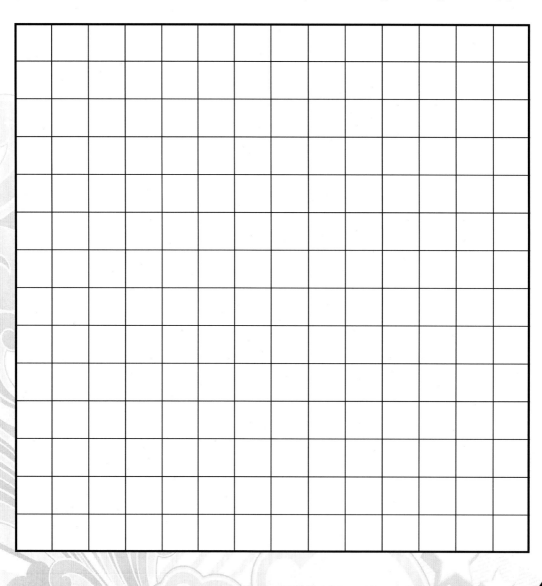

You bring me sunshine!

Write a letter telling someone why thinking about them always puts a warm and positive smile on your face.

Other amusing writing activities

Creativity

And now for something completely different…

Really useful invention

Pop song

Mini-me

Incredible me!

YOU magazine

200-word life story

Objectivity

Inspired

Slogan badges

Talent show

Now that's interesting!

Red-letter day

Dinner party debate

Time traveller

Publicity planner

Festival fun

Thanks a bunch!

An alphabet of gratitude

The unwish list

Adventures in wonderland

Superhero!

Postcard from Wowness

Art guide

Wondertour!

Creativity

> *Why should we all use our creative power? Because there is nothing that makes people so generous, joyful, lively, bold and compassionate.*
>
> *(Ueland, 1938, p155)*

Creativity often involves positive cognitive, emotional and social experiences such as being interested in something and exploring its possibilities; being inspired to try new ideas and techniques; feeling good about what we've created; and being encouraged and appreciated by others, for example. And when we experience positive emotions they may also help to create the space and desire for more creativity (Fredrickson, 2009).

The ability to be creative may also help people to become more flexible, resourceful and inventive in times when life is challenging, painful and difficult. Participating in creative activities on a regular basis may help to promote positive mental health (Cropley, 1990; Schmid, 2005).

The following ideas are designed to encourage and nurture creative thinking and expression in a wide range of contexts.

And now for something completely different...

Choose one of the objects from the list below (or pick one of your own) and think of 10 unusual and different ways you could use it. For example, you could use a wellington boot as a plant pot, or a bucket, or an umbrella stand, or tie a handle on it and use it as a bag, or you could fill it with presents instead of using a Christmas stocking.

an empty jam jar   a long stick   a wellington boot

a ball of wool   a large rock   an old pair of jeans

a newspaper   a sock.

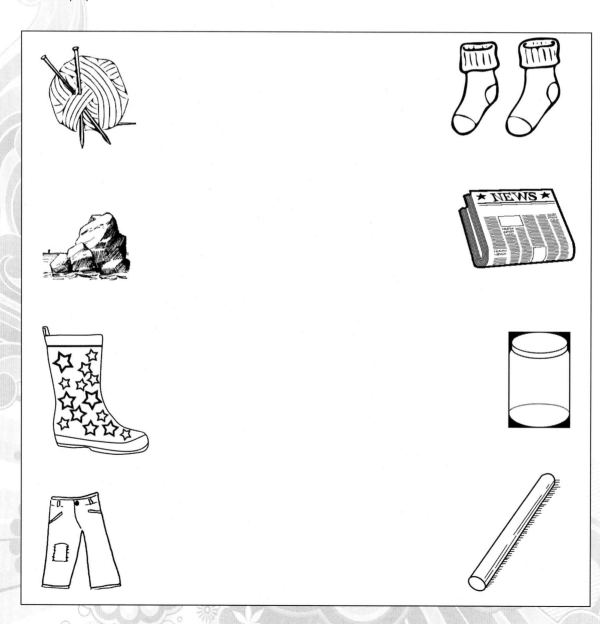

Wordsmith

Invent three words that you think our language needs. Then write a dictionary-style definition for each one of them. They can be funny, serious, useful, or crazy.

If you're doing this in a group, write out each of your words again on a separate card and their definitions on another set of cards. Shuffle everyone's words together and everyone's definitions together and see if you can match them up again.

Dictionary

WORD	Explanation

Animal discoverer

Imagine you work for a wildlife organisation and you find an animal that no one has ever seen before. For three days you watch it carefully, discovering everything you can about the creature. Fill in the following report to send back to your organisation so that your exciting discovery can be recorded.

Date of discovery:	
Discovered by:	
Location of discovery:	
Description of animal's appearance (size, shape, colour, etc):	
Sketch or photo of animal:	
General habitat (eg jungle, desert, mountain, river, etc):	
Description of nest or den:	
Types of food eaten:	
How it moves around:	
Sounds made by animal:	
Unusual behavioural characteristics:	
Precautions that need to be taken when approaching this animal:	

Really useful invention

Design a machine that your home really needs. It can be as wonderful and impossible as you like, but it has to help solve a real problem in your home. Maybe it's a finding-things machine, or a making-packed-lunches machine, or a stopping-arguments machine.

Draw and/or write a description of your amazing machine and write a few sentences about the difference it would make to your home if you had such a machine.

If things could talk

Think of an object in your home that is older than you – it could even be your home itself . Imagine the kind of story this object could tell you if it could talk for five minutes. What is the most exciting adventure the object has had, or the most interesting thing it has seen or heard? Write a short conversation between you and the object.

Pop song

Imagine your favourite band or singer has asked you to write the lyrics for their next song. Write your song below. It doesn't have to rhyme, use real words, or even make sense. It may even help if you pick a tune you like and think of the words you could sing to fit the music.

If you're feeling courageous, you could even try singing it! You never know, it might be a number one hit!

Mini-me

Imagine you wake up tomorrow and you're only 15cm high, but you still have to do everything you normally do. Choose one of your daily tasks and write about how, for example, you would manage to cook the dinner, do your work, walk the dog, or dress your baby if you were shrunk for a day.

Speechmark

How to

You have been asked to write the step-by-step instructions for an unusual task because you've had more experience doing the job than anyone else in the world. Choose one of the following tasks and write a clear guide for others to follow:

- How to cut a dragon's toenails.
- How to camp on the moon.
- How to cross the Atlantic Ocean in a hot-air balloon.
- How to train a caterpillar to do somersaults.
- How to make a delicious spinach and beetroot gateau.

INSTRUCTION MANUAL

Putting yourself in the picture

Choose an interesting picture that shows at least one person. It can be a grand masterpiece, a photo from a newspaper or magazine, or even a poster, cartoon or advertisement.

Then imagine you are one of the people in the picture. What are you thinking about for the five minutes after the moment captured in the picture or photo (apart from your thoughts about having your portrait painted or your photo taken!).

Write your thoughts below. If possible, stick a small version of the picture in the frame provided, or describe the picture in some way.

Perfect puddings

The dessert called peach melba was created for Nellie Melba, an opera singer, and the pavlova was created for the ballerina Anna Pavlova. If you were a chef creating a new dessert in honour of a special person in your life, what would you make?

Write out a recipe or a description of the dessert. Sketch out its design, as well, if you like. Why not try making a similar dessert for the special person? You never know, people may still be eating it in a hundred years' time!

PUDDING RECIPE

Name: _____

Ingredients:
_____
_____
_____
_____
_____
_____
_____

Preparation:
_____
_____
_____
_____
_____
_____
_____
_____

Other creative writing activities

Just for fun!
Comedy critic
Rhyme time
The same letter story
Flipside story
The reverse alphabet story

Feel-good factor
Waves of peace

Hope for the best
I have a dream…
Change the world
Save me!
Postcard from the future
Future GPS

Incredible me!
YOU magazine
200-word life story
Objectivity

Inspired
Slogan badges
Bookworm
Inaugural speech

Now that's interesting!
Red-letter day
Dinner party debate
Time traveller
Publicity planner
Festival fun
Ideal home

Heartfelt
The perfect love letter
Love is…
If walls had ears…

Thanks a bunch!
Bon appetit!
Not flowers again!

Adventures in Wonderland
Superhero!
Postcard from Wowness
Art guide

Feel-good factor

It can never do any harm to think about the things that make us feel happy and calm.

The more we focus on happy, joyful, soothing and peaceful experiences, the more likely we are to feel happy, joyful, soothed and peaceful. When we feel happy in our own lives we may feel more energised, more hopeful and more likely to be generous and caring towards others.

The following writing activities will help you to explore happiness, joyfulness and peacefulness in different ways, enriching your experience of the feel-good factor.

Just another perfect day

Write the story of one of the best days you've ever had. Maybe something wonderful happened, or it was perfectly happy, or you enjoyed every minute, or it was life-changing? What was the best thing about your best day?

_____

_____

_____

_____

_____

_____

_____

_____

_____

_____

_____

_____

_____

_____

_____

_____

What was the best thing about your best day?

_____

_____

_____

If smiles could speak

A genuine smile can say all kinds of things – give the smiles on this page some positive words to speak, such as 'I like you!' or 'Thank you!' Next time you see a smile, wonder what it might be saying. What might your smiles be saying to those who see them?

My Smile might be saying......

Happy maps

Draw a map of three places where you've felt especially happy. Around each place write some words and phrases about your happiest memories there.

A few of my favourite things

Write down 10 things that make you feel happy and cheer you up. For example, they could be songs, TV shows, movies, memories, activities, food or people. Notice how you feel as you think about these happy things. What difference would it make to your life if you could experience one of these happy things every day?

The happiness experiment

Funnily enough, one of the best ways to feel happy is to make someone else happy! Choose three people – a family member, a friend and a complete stranger (like the bus driver, or a person sitting alone in a café, or someone who lives down your street that you've never spoken to).

For each person list several ways you could share a little bit of happiness with them.

Try one of these ideas and write about your happy experiment at the bottom of the page.

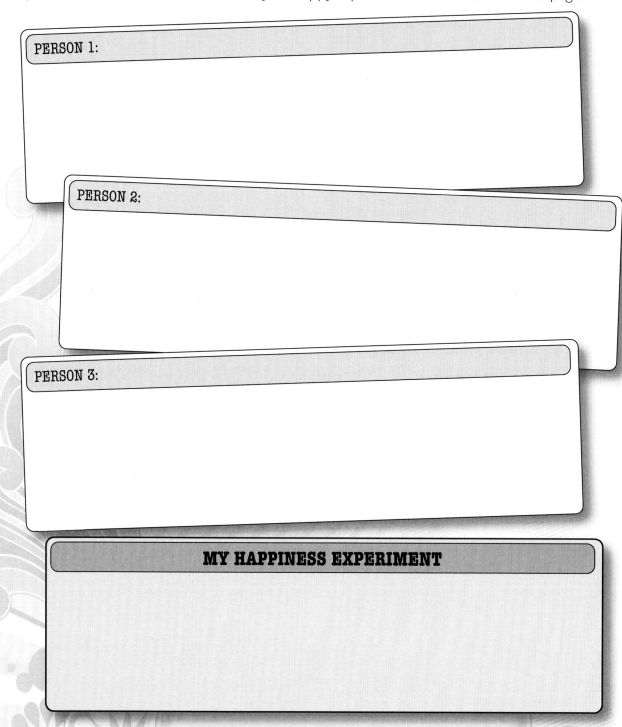

PERSON 1:

PERSON 2:

PERSON 3:

MY HAPPINESS EXPERIMENT

Happiness pizza

Imagine happiness is a pizza. It can have all kinds of ingredients and toppings! What are some of the ingredients of your happiest times? They might include family, friends, sunshine, beach, good food, ice cream, a long lie-in, a good book or running, for example. Write them in the different pizza toppings.

Do I have to?

Make a list of 10 things you've *had* to do so far today, such as get up, get washed, get dressed, clean your teeth, make breakfast, or things you'll *have* to do later, such as go shopping, make the dinner, walk the dog, or mend the car. Write them on the numbered lines below.

Then turn each of the things on your 'I *have* to do' list into a choice on your 'I choose to do list', and say why you choose to do it.

What difference does it make when you 'choose' to do the things you think you *have* to do?

My Have-to-do list	My Choose-to-do list
eg. I have to make breakfast for the family	eg. I choose to make breakfast for my family because I love them and don't want them to go hungry.
1.	1.
2.	2.
3.	3.
4.	4.
5.	5.
6.	6.
7.	7.
8.	8.
9.	9.
10.	10.

Waves of peace

Listen to some peaceful music or find a peaceful place. Write any peaceful thoughts, ideas and images you have on the waves below.

Comfort blanket

Design a blanket covered in encouraging words, soothing sayings, and comforting thoughts. When would you most like to snuggle under this blanket?

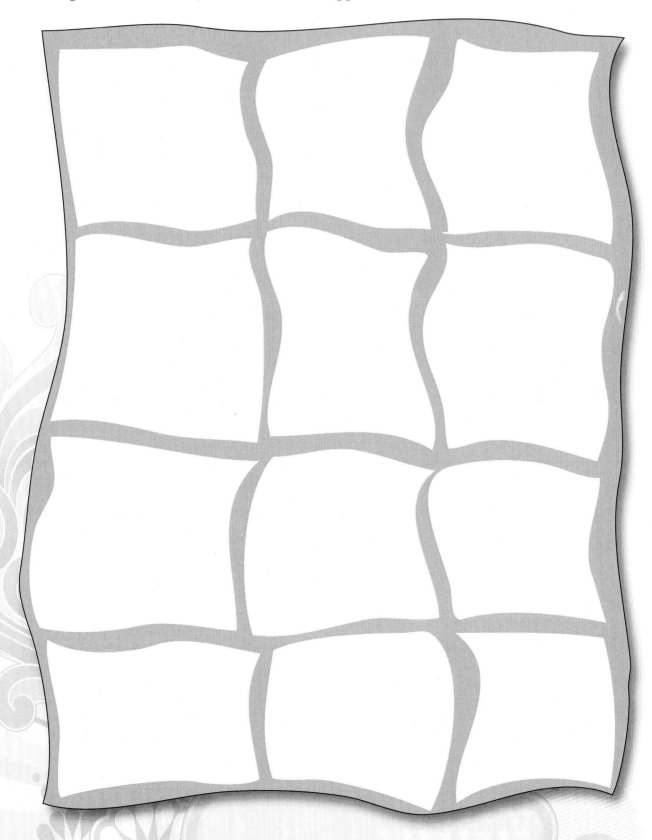

Supporters' Club

Think of a challenging, worrying or confusing situation that you're facing at the moment. Write it in the spiky shape in the middle of the page. Think of the people who care most about you. In the speech bubbles, write the words they'd say to help you, encourage you, support you and comfort you if they were here with you.

Other happy and feel-good writing activities

Just for fun!
The funniest thing!

Smile file

Word search

You bring me sunshine!

Hope for the best
Rainbow of hope

I have a dream…

Change the world

Booster pack

Postcard from the future

Good news

Future GPS

Worry manager

Incredible me!
Treasured words

Best friend

To the world, with love from me

Expert witnesses

Inspired
Inspirational balloons

Make a difference

Talent show

Birthday letter

Now that's interesting!
Red-letter day

Worthy cause

Heartfelt
The perfect love letter

Love is…

31 things I like about you

Home-building

SMS

Caring hands

The kindness effect

It's the thought that counts!

If walls had ears…

Future friends

Thanks a bunch!
An alphabet of gratitude

Thank you card

The unwish list

Bon appetit!

Thanks everyone!

A whole houseful!

Family appreciation

Thankful for me

Not flowers again!

Adventures in Wonderland
Body wonderful!

Superhero!

Postcard from Wowness

Wondertour!

Hope for the best

Hopefulness and optimism are important to our mental health because they help us to believe that life is worth living and that difficult things will improve, go away, change or be resolved. When there is no hope life can feel desperate, meaningless and sad. When we feel hopeful and optimistic we are more likely to persevere when we're faced with a challenge. We are more likely to search for and try different solutions and possibilities. We are also more likely to succeed at the things we do, set ourselves goals and work towards them, feel good about ourselves, and have better health and relationships (Snyder, 2002; Pettit, 2004).

Sometimes hopefulness and optimism can be lost in the clutter and pressure of the moment and the everyday, so it is important to pin it down, and wonder about it, and explore what it means to our lives so that it can become real and tangible again.

The following activities include some creative ways to explore hopefulness, and one to help manage a worry.

Rainbow of hope

Using coloured pens or crayons create a rainbow of hopefulness on the page below with the following themes:

- Red – my realistic hopes for the future.
- Orange – my optimistic thoughts.
- Yellow – yells (cheers) – things my friends would shout to cheer me on.
- Green – great things I've done.
- Blue – beautiful things/people that inspire me.
- Purple – people who love me, support me and believe in me.

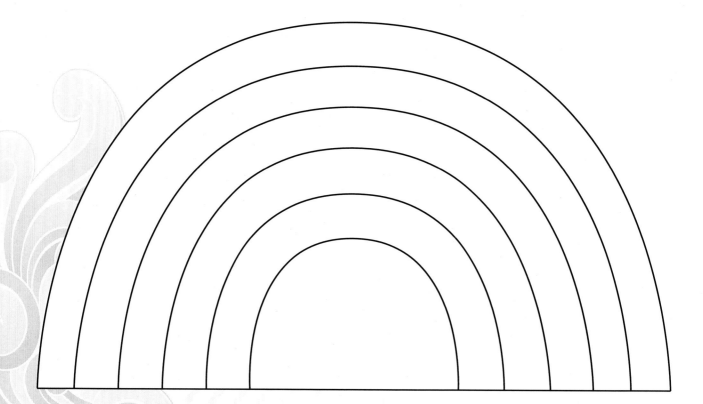

I have a dream...

What are your dreams for your life? Write about the best dream you have for your future. List three things you could do to help your dream come true.

Change the world

If you could discover, invent or create one thing that would change the world for the better, what would you like to create and why? Write an imaginary press report or newspaper article about your amazing discovery.

Hope letter

Write a letter to a child you know. Be encouraging, notice what they are doing well, and tell them your hopes for their future. Imagine you actually sent the letter. What difference might it make to the child's life? What difference would it have made to your life if someone had sent you a letter like this?

To: _____   **From:** _____

_____

_____

_____

_____

_____

_____

_____

_____

_____

_____

_____

_____

_____

_____

_____

Save me!

Imagine the world could speak for five minutes. What would our planet like to say to help us look after it better?

Booster pack

Think about a time when you felt discouraged. Write a list of 10 things that would have given you hope and energised you at that time. Keep the list safe to encourage you again in the future.

My Booster list

1.

2.

3.

4.

5.

6.

7.

8.

9.

10.

Postcard from the future

Imagine that you take a trip to your future life, 10 years from now, and you're really enjoying yourself. Write yourself a postcard from the future saying what you like best about your future life and what you did to help make your future turn out so well.

Choose a picture for the postcard – draw one yourself or find a suitable picture to stick on it.

Good news

Find a newspaper and look for three pieces of good news that help you to feel optimistic. Maybe you'll find your good news in the weather forecast; the sports pages; information about the latest medical research; a missing person who was found safe and well; or even an advert about a sale in your favourite store!

Once you've found three pieces of good news, summarise them in the spaces below and rate them according to how hopeful they make you feel on a scale of 1–5, where 5 is very hopeful.

Future GPS

Imagine that you have a GPS (car-directing system) to guide you into the future. It will tell you which is the best way to go, where to stop, which way to turn, and which roads to avoid. For example, you can programme it for the fastest route (but that's usually on uninteresting highways and motorways) or for the shortest route (which can take you down side streets or pretty lanes). Or you can avoid certain features, like town centres, bridges, tolls, ferries and motorways.

How would you like to programme your journey into the future? What would you like to avoid, or include, along the way? If your future GPS could speak, what are some of the directions you think it would give you so that you arrive safe and happy where you'd like to be in five years' time?

Programme features:

○ Fastest route
○ Shortest route
○ Scenic route
○ Fuel-saving route
○ Other type of route (specify)
○ Avoiding (specify)
○ Via (specify)

Worry manager

It's natural to have concerns about the future, from niggling little thoughts, to fears about major disasters. Choose one of your moderate-sized worries and write about it on the page below. How does this exercise help your worries to feel more manageable?

On a scale of 0-10 where is 0 is not worried at all and 10 is extremely worried my worry is

0 1 2 3 4 5 6 7 8 9 10

My worry or concern stops me from enjoying life as much as I want because

My worry or concern helps me in some way by

Other people could help me to worry less by

Three things I can do that will help me to worry less about this are

1.

2.

3.

Looking at the scale at the top of the section, one thing I can do to move my worry to the next number lower in the scale is

If I wasn't so worried about this I could

Thinking about my worry in this way has given me more hope because

Other writing activities that may inspire hopefulness

Feel-good factor
Comfort blanket
Supporters' Club

Inspired
Inspirational balloons
Talent show
Birthday letter

Heartfelt
The perfect love letter
Future friends

Thanks a bunch!
Thankful for me
Wondertour!

Incredible me!

Each person is a unique and complex blend of characteristics, skills, interests, personality traits, thoughts, values, ideas and achievements. It's important for every person to feel good about themselves and to value their special qualities and achievements. It's also useful to stop and think about the positive contributions they make to their friends, family members and communities, and to reflect on how others value them. When people feel proud of themselves and their achievements they are more likely to persist when faced with a challenging task (Williams & DeSteno, 2008).

The following activities are designed to help writers explore their uniqueness in positive ways, to highlight their value to others, and to focus on thoughts and ideas that build them up and encourage them.

YOU magazine

Create a contents page for a magazine that focuses on your specific range of interests – the food, music, activities and hobbies, and so on, that you like the best. Write a sentence about each feature that would inspire someone else to be interested too.

YOU

Issue date:

Editor:

Treasured words

All kinds of messages float around in our heads – some of them are useful and some of them are just annoying, discouraging or hurtful. Inside the treasure box, write some of the helpful and encouraging messages that pop into your thoughts. On the bin, write some of the unhelpful thoughts that pop into your head. When you've finished writing, tear off the bin section and throw it away. Keep the words that you treasure.

Speechmark

Best friend

Write a radio-style advert for yourself as a good friend. Create a snappy jingle for the advert and make sure it highlights your best features as a friend.

And this award goes to...

Create a certificate for yourself that celebrates one of your proudest moments or greatest accomplishments. It may even be something that only you know about. Describe why you were given this award and what helped you to achieve it.

This award is to

_____

in celebration of achieving

_____

This was achieved for the following reasons:

_____

_____

_____

_____

_____

_____

_____

_____

_____

_____

To the world, with love from me

You are a unique gift to the world. No one else has your blend of gifts, strengths, ideas, interests and skills. Write a list of five different gifts you give to the world. Write your name on the gift tag.

'To the world, with love from

Expert witnesses

Choose three people who have witnessed you doing something well. Imagine a journalist has just called them up and asked them what your strengths are. What would each of them say? Write the journalist's notes on the notebook pages below.

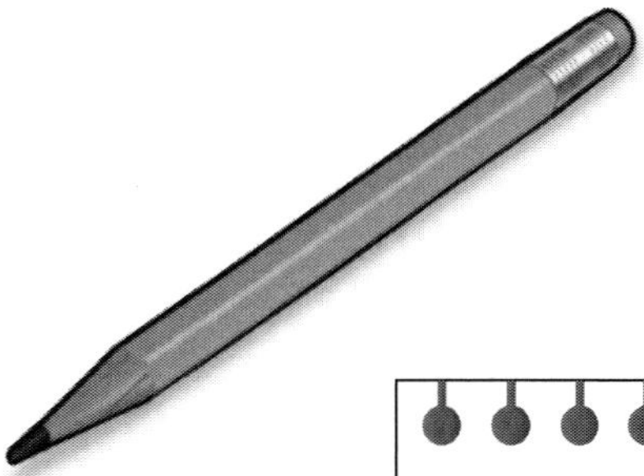

Name: _____

Name: _____

Name: _____

200-word life story

Write the story of your life in 200 words. What did you include and why? What did you leave out and why?

_____

_____

_____

_____

_____

_____

_____

_____

_____

_____

_____

_____

_____

_____

_____

_____

_____

_____

Crisis management

Think about a challenge you have faced in your life, especially one you managed well. It can be as simple as a practical task, like changing the oil in your car, or a complicated emotional challenge, such as coping with a crisis. Write a short leaflet to help someone who's facing the same challenge you faced. What useful tips could you pass on to others?

My *real* job description

Ever felt like the things you do in your work don't quite match up to your job description? Here's the chance to put the record straight and write a job description for the things you really do in your day. Even if you're not officially employed, you are still doing other things. Or write a job description for the job you'd really like to do.

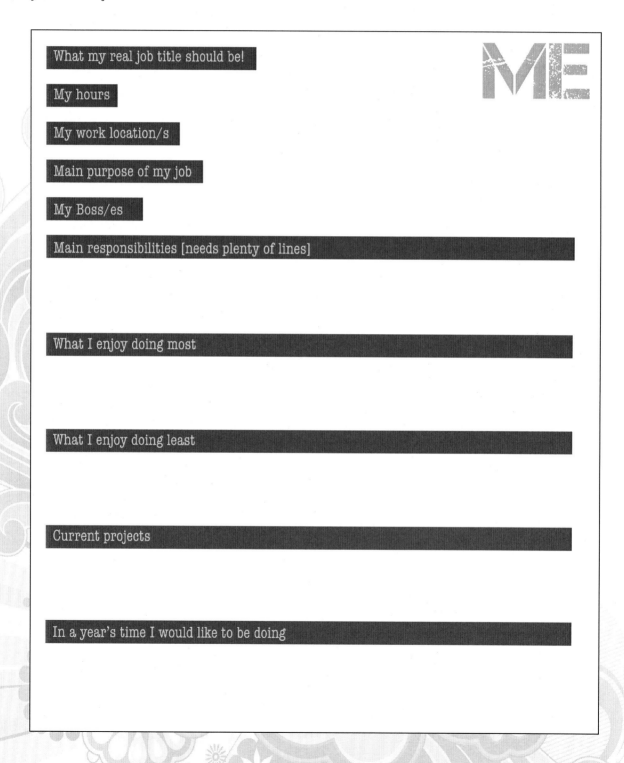

What my real job title should be!

My hours

My work location/s

Main purpose of my job

My Boss/es

Main responsibilities [needs plenty of lines]

What I enjoy doing most

What I enjoy doing least

Current projects

In a year's time I would like to be doing

ME

Objectivity

A local museum has chosen several people from the community, including you, to tell the story of their lives through six objects. Which objects will you choose and what will you write on the cards that explain them? You are allowed 30 words per card.

Fill in the cards below so that the museum staff can have them printed.

Object: _____
I chose this object because
_____
_____
_____
_____

Object: _____
I chose this object because
_____
_____
_____
_____

Object: _____
I chose this object because
_____
_____
_____
_____

Object: _____
I chose this object because
_____
_____
_____
_____

Object: _____
I chose this object because
_____
_____
_____
_____

Object: _____
I chose this object because
_____
_____
_____
_____

Other writing tasks that may encourage self-worth

Just for fun!
Word search

Creativity
How to

Feel-good factor
The happiness experiment
Do I *have* to?
Supporters' Club

Hope for the best
Change the world
Hope letter
Booster pack
Postcard from the future
Worry manager

Inspired
Make a difference
Talent show

Now that's interesting!
Worthy cause
It's the law
Local knowledge
Publicity planner

Heartfelt
The perfect love letter
Love is…
SMS
The kindness effect
If walls had ears…
Future friends

Thanks a bunch!
An alphabet of gratitude
Thankful for me

Adventures in Wonderland
Body wonderful!
Superhero!

Inspired

Inspiration is something that can happen when we see another human being doing something amazing and it sparks our own desire to strive for excellence. Such inspiration may come from famous leaders, faith teachings, experts and champions, our teacher, colleagues, heroes, parents, friends and even from our own children. We may be inspired when we watch an Olympic gymnast perform a graceful and powerful floor routine, when we hear a rousing political speech, when we gaze on an amazing picture, or when a toddler stops to comfort another child who's lost her teddy.

Inspiration is most useful when it transforms our lives in some way, when it challenges us to make a real difference, and when it encourages us to strive for something better in our own lives, work and relationships.

The following activities are designed to help writers explore the people and things that have inspired them, or that could inspire them in the future.

Inspirational balloons

Inspiring thoughts are those that lift us up (like helium balloons) and help us to be better people in some way. They may inspire us to be unselfish, generous, kind or persevering. Or they give us hope, and the glimmer of light at the end of the tunnel, when times are challenging, painful, lonely or sad.

What are some of the inspirational comments, messages, thoughts, verses or songs, for example, that encourage you to be a better person, or to have hope in the dark places?

Write your favourite inspiring thoughts on the balloons.

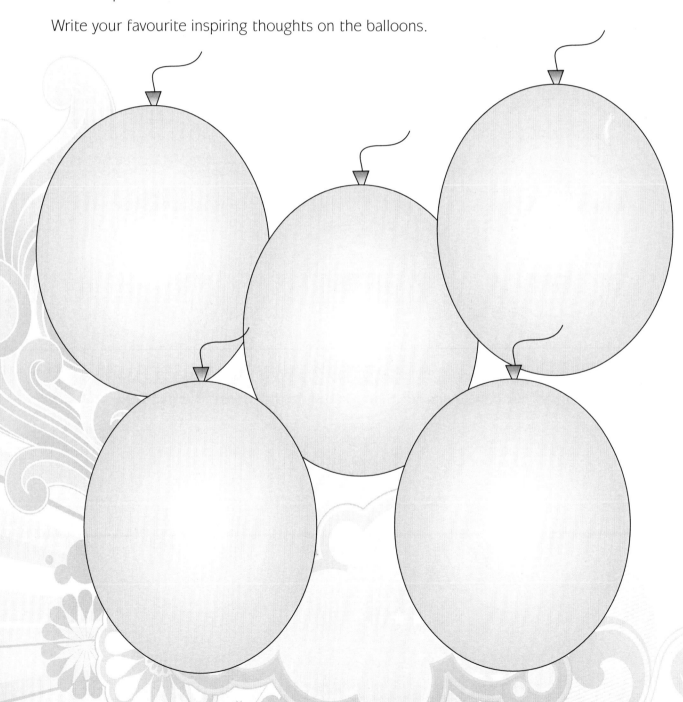

Emergency kit

A natural disaster is about to destroy your home. You can take one suitcase of things for your basic needs (clothes, money, a little food and emergency supplies). You must also take a shopping bag with three items for you to use to help other people who are in need. What three things would you put in your shopping bag and why?

Slogan badges

Write some catchy slogans for the badges below. Each slogan must inspire others to think of something they could do to make the world a better, happier or more peaceful place.

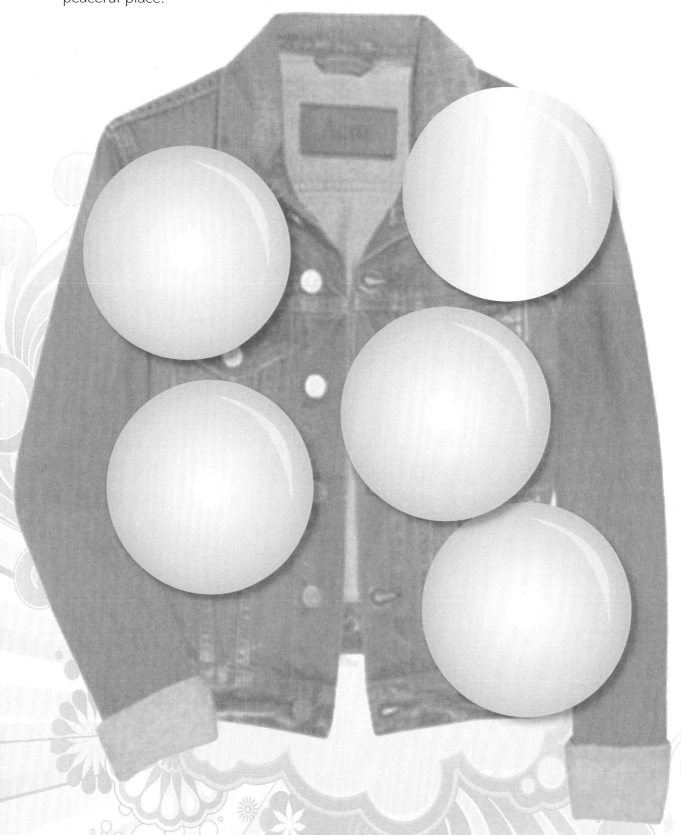

Brave-Heart

Think of the bravest person that you know well, such as a friend or family member. Imagine that you're nominating them for an award. You're allowed to write up to 200 words to convince the judges that your friend should win the award.

Write your competition entry on the form below.

Bravest person award goes to

Watch my face

Many of us look at our watches or clocks several times a day. Think of some sentences you could engrave on watch faces that would encourage or inspire people to live their lives well in some way. For example, one man gave his son-in-law a watch on the day he married his daughter. On the watch face was engraved, 'Say something kind to Sarah today.' What other messages would be good to engrave on a watch or clock face? Write two or three of them on the faces below.

Bookworm

Write a book review for the most inspiring book you've ever read. Include in your review the difference that reading this book has made to your life or the way that you think.

BOOK REVIEW

BOOK TITLE:

inaugural speech

Imagine that you have just been elected prime minister or president of your country. You need to make a speech that will inspire your nation. What would be your opening lines to catch people's attention; your main three points; and your inspiring conclusion?

PRIME MINISTER'S SPEECH

Make a difference

Your school or employer is part of a charitable foundation committed to making a difference in the world. Each person has to spend two weeks doing something somewhere in the world to make a positive difference to another person's life, to a community or to the environment. You can choose where you will go and what you would like to do.

Write a proposal in 300 words telling your employer or head teacher:

- what project you want to do

- why you have chosen this project

- what difference your work will make to the person, community or the environment

- what difference this project will make to your life, too.

Talent show

Your friends have submitted you for a TV talent show. It's for any kind of talent, not necessarily a public performance – just something your friends think you're really good at that isn't dangerous in any way! It can even be knitting, making pizza or breeding hamsters! You have to demonstrate your talent for up to five minutes on TV and three very kind judges will say what they liked best about what you did and give you a prize of one thing (perhaps paying for a course, or a trainer, or buying some equipment, for example) that will help you develop your talent even further.

Write on the TV screen below what you'd do for five minutes. Write some specific and thoughtfully encouraging words from each of the judges. In the gift box, write what you would like your prize to be that will help you develop your talent further.

Speechmark

Birthday letter

It's your child's 12th birthday and you want to write them a letter to inspire them and to help them get through the challenging teenage years. You want them to be safe, happy, have good relationships and work towards the important goals they have for their life.

What will you write that will inspire your child?

HAPPY BIRTHDAY

HAPPY
BIRTHDAY

12
TODAY

Other writing tasks that may be inspiring

Creativity
How to

Feel-good factor
The happiness experiment
Do I *have* to?
Waves of peace
Comfort blanket
Supporters' Club

Hope for the best
Rainbow of hope
I have a dream…
Change the world
Hope letter
Save me!
Booster pack
Postcard from the future
Good news
Future GPS
Worry manager

Incredible me!
Treasured words
Best friend
And this award goes to…
To the world, with love from me
Expert witnesses
Crisis management

Now that's interesting!
The big questions
Worthy cause
It's the law

Heartfelt
The perfect love letter
Love is…
SMS
The kindness effect
It's the thought that counts!
Future friends

Thanks a bunch!
An alphabet of gratitude
Thank you card
Family appreciation
Thankful for me

Adventures in Wonderland
My hero!
Naturally amazing
Starry, starry night
Body wonderful!
Man-made wonders
Small but significant
Superhero!
Postcard from Wowness

Now that's interesting

As soon as we are born we begin to explore our world and look for new things to stimulate our senses and our thoughts. We are curious creatures and we become engrossed in interesting stories, fascinated by unusual discoveries, stimulated by new challenges, and determined to develop new skills.

'Interesting' is the opposite to 'boring'. When we're bored we become uninterested and listless and our mood may flatten. When we're interested in something our senses are awakened, we are re-energised, up for a challenge, ready to focus on something new, ready to learn and expand our thoughts.

All kinds of things interest us and each person is interested in different things. So it is up to you to find something interesting on the following pages, or to make something interesting out of whatever you discover.

Explore.

Red-letter experience

Choose something you've always wanted to do, but you haven't had the chance to try yet. Perhaps it's a new hobby, an exciting sport, speaking another language, living abroad, going on a world cruise. Imagine that you win a day, a week or a month to do this activity.

Write a diary page about your experience. What did you like the best? What was the most difficult part? What was different to your expectations? What was your happiest moment?

Dinner party debate

Imagine you're having a private party and you can invite six famous people to dinner. They can be from any time in history and any place in the world. Write each of them a place card with their name on it and add three interesting questions you'd like to ask them. Then wonder about what their answers might be and write some possibilities on their speech bubbles.

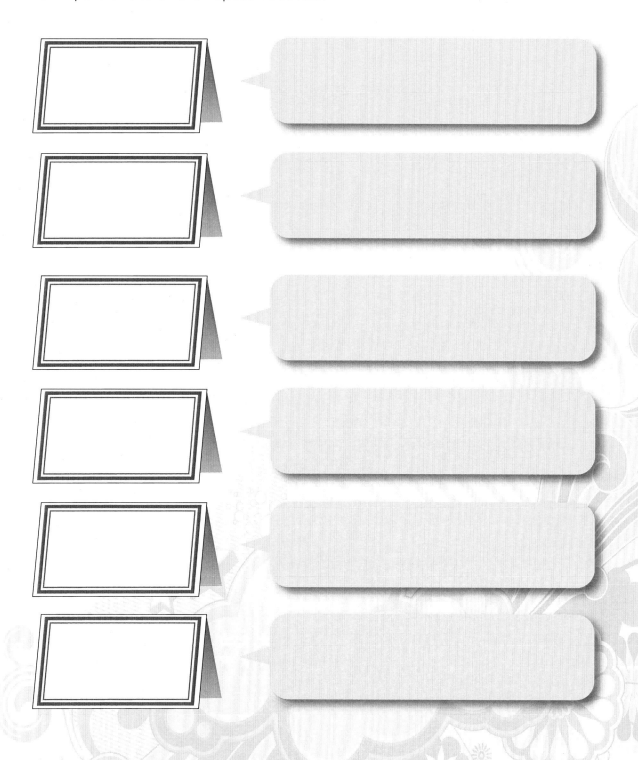

The big questions

Write down three BIG questions you'd really like to know the answers to. Then make up your own possible answers for your questions. If you're in a group, try swapping your questions with each other and make up answers for each other's questions.

1

Q

A

2

Q

A

3

Q

A

Worthy cause

You've been asked to start a charity or action group that will make a positive difference to your community. You could offer help for people with special needs; help a minority or oppressed group express their wishes and concerns; or promote something that will make a difference to your environment or community, such as better recycling facilities, or a pedestrian crossing over a dangerous road.

What good cause would you like to start? What would you do? How would you encourage others to help you? What difference would it make to your community and people's lives?

Name of your charity or group

Aims of your group

How will you find your group?

What do you plan to do?

What creative ideas do you have for publicising the group?

What equipment and skills will you need to help you get started?

What's the biggest difference you hope this group will make?

Time traveller

Imagine that you can travel back in time, to any place in the world, and live there for a month. Maybe you'd be an explorer, or an Egyptian nobleperson, or a pioneer on the American prairie. Maybe you'd be a soldier in World War 1, a sailor in an old ship, a lady from a Jane Austen novel, or the first person on the moon.

Who would you choose to be and where would you live? What would you find difficult if you lived in another time or place? What would you enjoy the most?

I'd choose to be

I'd live in

The things I would find difficult about living as that person in that time would be

The things I would enjoy the most about being that person in that time would be

It's the law

You've won a competition by writing the idea for a law that the judges decided would improve the safety and well-being of most of the people in your country. It will also be named after you.

What new law did you write, why did you choose that law, and what difference do you think it will make to your community?

My law is called

APPROVED

I chose this law because

The difference it will make to my community is

Local knowledge

A travel website has invited you to write a review of three places within 10 miles of where you live: a restaurant; a tourist attraction; and somewhere that's fun for a family outing or picnic.

Choose three places you know well, and write your reviews below. Write what you like and don't like about each place. Include at least one 'insider tip', something that you know because you're local – like special discount days and the best desserts to choose. Then give each place a rating by colouring in the stars, where five stars mean that it is excellent and one means that it is not worth visiting.

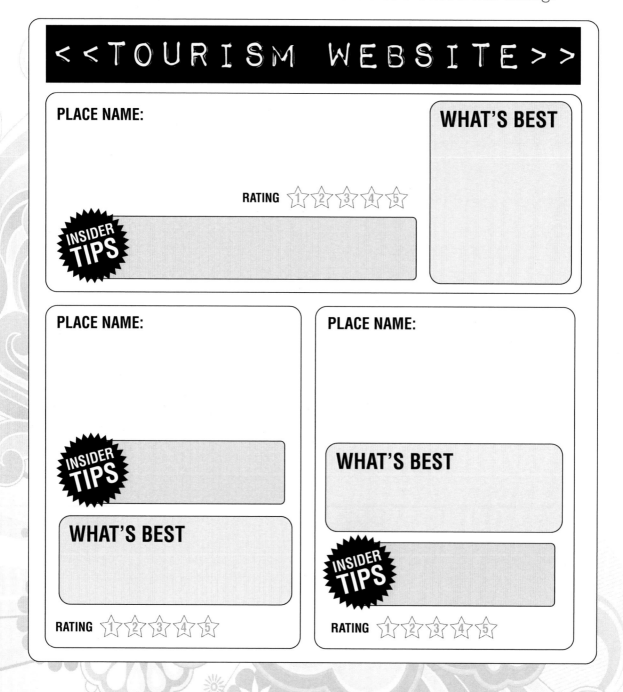

Publicity planner

One of your friends has started a business and they need you to come up with some cheap and easy ways to promote it.

Choose a business of any kind. Think of the target customers, and then devise three creative and low-cost plans to promote the business. You can use the internet, Twitter, Facebook and any other safe, thoughtful and legal way to promote your friend's business, such as writing a message in the sand on the beach. For example, if your friend has an ice-cream van you could put out a tweet about 'Flip-Flop Friday!' where everyone who comes to buy an ice cream wearing flip-flops and saying the password 'Flip-Flop Friday' will get a free chocolate flake in their ice cream!

Festival fun

Imagine you're part of a team who want to create a new national holiday. You have to decide what you're going to celebrate, when the holiday will be, what traditions you want to start, and so on.

Use the page below to explore your ideas and prepare you to explain them to the rest of the team.

NEW NATIONAL HOLIDAY

_____

_____

_____

_____

_____

_____

_____

_____

_____

_____

_____

_____

_____

_____

_____

_____

_____

_____

_____

Ideal home

You've been looking online for a new home, and suddenly you find the perfect place. It has everything you ever wanted in a house! And it's the perfect price in the perfect location!

Write the seller's detailed description of the house, taking each room in turn. If you're stuck, look at some estate agents' brochures or websites to give you some ideas.

General description of type of property, its age and location, and so on

FOR SALE

External (gardens and garage, etc)

Hallway

Lounge

Dining room

Kitchen

Utility room

Bathroom

Master bedroom

Bedroom 2

Bedroom 3

Other rooms (studio, attic, gym, games room, music room, craft room, nursery, etc)

Other special features

Other interesting writing tasks

Just for fun!

Comedy critic

The same letter story

Flipside story

The reverse alphabet story

Creativity

And now for something completely different…

Wordsmith

Animal discoverer

Really useful invention

If things could talk

Mini-me

How to

Putting yourself in the picture

Perfect puddings

Feel-good factor

The happiness experiment

Hope for the best

Change the world

Save me!

Good news

Incredible me!

YOU magazine

200-word life story

Crisis management

Objectivity

Inspired

Emergency kit

Bookworm

Inaugural speech

Make a difference

Heartfelt

The kindness effect

Thanks a bunch!

An alphabet of gratitude

Bon appetit!

Thanks everyone!

A whole houseful!

Glad you made it!

Not flowers again!

Adventures in Wonderland

My hero!

Naturally amazing

Man-made wonders

Small but significant

Superhero!

Art guide

Wondertour!

Heartfelt

Love is one of the most significant and basic human emotions. When we feel loved we often experience other positive emotions and we feel happier, safer, braver and valued. When we love other people we become more courageous, less selfish, kinder, and happier.

Various research studies suggest that some of the best ways to feel happier and healthier are by helping other people to feel happy and loved, and by doing and saying kind and caring things (Hamilton, 2010).

The following activities can be used to explore different aspects of being loved and feeling cared for, as well as different ways in which we can love and care for others.

The perfect love letter

Write yourself a love letter. Think of a person who loves or loved you the most – or invent a person – the most loving person you can think of. Imagine this person knows your deepest thoughts, your secret feelings and everything about you, and still loves you 100 per cent. Write a letter to yourself from this person – loving, encouraging, accepting, forgiving, hoping, believing the best, and saying the words you really long to hear.

Love is...

What does love mean to you? Think of all the words and phrases that describe good, happy, positive love and fill the heart below with as many as possible.

31 things I like about you

Write a list of 31 things you like or appreciate about someone close to you. Find a way to tell them a different one of these things every day for a month. You can tell them face-to-face, text them, email them, or leave them a note, for example. Then write a few sentences about the effect this has on your relationship.

1	2	3	4	5
6	7	8	9	10
11	12	13	14	15
16	17	18	19	20
21	22	23	24	25
26	27	28	29	30
31				

Home-building

What makes a house into a place where you feel at home? Write one idea inside each of the house shapes below. What one thing could you do to make your house even more of a home for the people who live there?

SMS

Think of three people you love. Imagine that each person texts you to remind you about something special you did that made them feel really loved.

Write each of their texts on one of the phone screens below.

Caring hands

Think about some of the kindest things anyone has ever done for you and write them on the left hand below.

Then think of some of the kindest things you've done for other people and write them on the right hand.

Underneath the hands write three kind things you could do for other people in the next week.

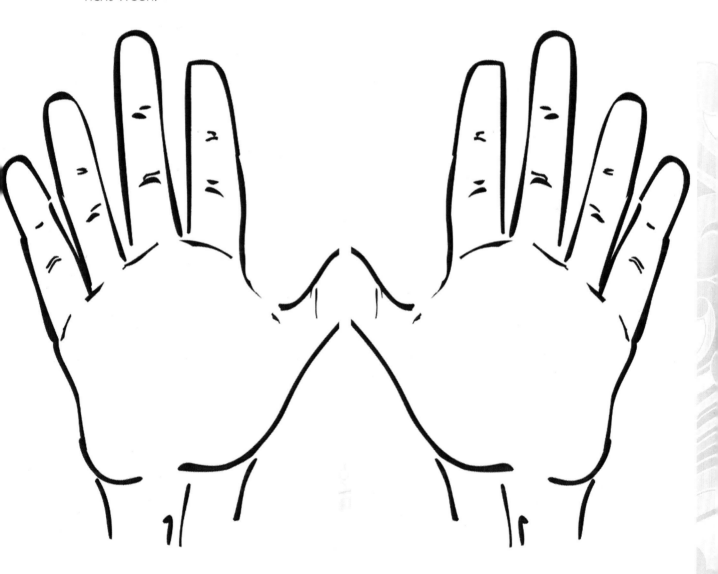

The kindness effect

Think of something kind you did for a complete stranger. It can be as simple as giving up your seat for them, or smiling at them. Write an imaginary story about the way your kind act might have transformed their life.

KINDNESS

It's the thought that counts!

Make a list of the people who are most important to you. Imagine you are giving each of them a gift that would make an enormous difference to their life. It can be anything, even things money can't buy. The gift could be a plane ticket to see a distant relative, or their health again if they have been really ill… Write the gift you'd like to give them next to their name. Maybe you could find a way to let them know what you'd like to give them, even if you can't… Remember, it's the thought that counts!

NAME	GIFT

If walls had ears...

What if the walls in your home have been listening to everything that's gone on in your home? And what if the walls of your home could speak to you? The walls are there to protect you and be supportive. So what are the protective, helpful and supportive things the walls in your house might like to say to you? Write some of your ideas on the bricks below.

Future friends

Imagine your friends have come together, ten years from now, to plan a surprise birthday party for you. What do you think they'll be saying about you as a friend? Write some of their conversation on the speech bubbles below.

Other possible warm-hearted writing activities

Just for fun!
You bring me sunshine!

Feel-good factor
If smiles could speak

The happiness experiment

Comfort blanket

Supporters' Club

Hope for the best
Change the world

Hope letter

Booster pack

Incredible me!
Treasured words

Best friend

To the world, with love from me

Crisis management

Inspired
Brave-Heart

Make a difference

Birthday letter

Now that's interesting!
Worthy cause

Thanks a bunch!
Thank you card

Thanks everyone!

Family appreciation

Thankful for me

Not flowers again!

Thanks a bunch!

A sense of gratitude, for even the simplest things in our lives, can transform our thoughts. It fills our lives with a sense of positive appreciation towards those who have given us things, cared for us, provided for us, or even invented the everyday things that make our lives today much easier than a hundred years ago. Without gratitude and appreciation we fall into the muddy rut of taking very important people and things for granted, robbing both us, and those who have provided for us, of positive experiences.

Bill O'Hanlon, world-famous psychotherapist, thinks thankfulness is so important that he encourages people to think of 25 specific things to be thankful for before breakfast (O'Hanlon, 2011). Having a thankful attitude can help people to feel happier, more content and healthier. It can even help us to have better relationships with others, and to overcome challenges and negative thinking patterns. Gratitude is a positive attitude, and positivity can help open our minds to new ideas, possibilities and relationships.

The following writing activities focus on different aspects of gratitude.

An alphabet of gratitude

Write at least one thing you're thankful for beginning with each letter of the alphabet. If you're feeling especially ambitious or grateful, try writing three things per letter. How many did you find in the end?

A	**B**	**C**	**D**
E	**F**	**G**	**H**
I	**J**	**K**	**L**
M	**N**	**O**	**P**
Q	**R**	**S**	**T**
U	**V**	**W**	**X**
	Y	**Z**	

Thank you card

Choose one person who's made a significant and positive difference in your life. Write a note of appreciation to them in the thank you card below. Maybe you could send them a real thank you card? What might it mean to them if you did?

JUST TO SAY

THANK YOU

The unwish list

Write a list of 20 objects that you'd never want to own, and write why you wouldn't want to have them. Be thankful for your un-possessions!

Bon appetit!

Make a list of the food ingredients you like the best – the ones for which you're really grateful! Then design a five-course meal using as many of these ingredients as possible. Write out a descriptive and tantalising menu below. Then imagine you're slowly eating each of the dishes. Mmm, delicious! What are your top three favourite ingredients?

Menu

Ingredients

Starters

Main Course

Dessert

Thanks everyone!

Choose something that you're wearing, or something that you have in your pocket or your bag. Then think of all the people who've been involved with making and transporting and selling the item. Think of all the different parts and how they were grown, designed, mined, woven, processed, made, transported, and so on. Imagine all the different workers you can think of who may have been involved in making and handling the object and list them below. Make sure you don't leave anyone out! That's a lot of people to thank for your pair of jeans, trainers, watch, handbag or sandwich!

ITEM NAME

PARTS OF THE ITEM

PEOPLE INVOLVED IN THE PRODUCTION PROCESS

A whole houseful!

Imagine you're walking through some of the rooms in your house. In each room you must find 10 things you're most thankful for before you move into the next room, or the garage, the garden, or even the garden shed! If you live in one room, think about each cupboard, drawer, shelf, and so on, instead. Not sure how thankful you are for something? Imagine life without it and see what happens.

Draw a simple plan of your home or room below, including the main rooms or storage areas. Then list the things you're most thankful for in each area.

Family appreciation

On the tree below write the names of some of the people in your family that you know the best. Think about the different things they've given you that couldn't be bought, or wrapped in a box, such as teaching you how to fish; showing you how to play a game; encouraging you towards a goal; sharing an important piece of wisdom with you; making sacrifices for you; or inspiring you to do something well. Write some of the gifts each person has given you under their names. How could you thank them for giving you these very important gifts?

Speechmark

Thankful for me

We sometimes wish we were someone else, but often those people aren't as happy as we imagine them to be. Write a few thoughts about why you're thankful that you are you, alive and here in this world today.

Glad you made it!

Think of an invention you couldn't live without. Maybe it's your car, dishwasher, the internet, your laptop, phone, bed, TV, hot shower, or even a humble light bulb. Write an email to the inventor of your favourite invention, telling them how much you appreciate their invention and the difference it makes to your life.

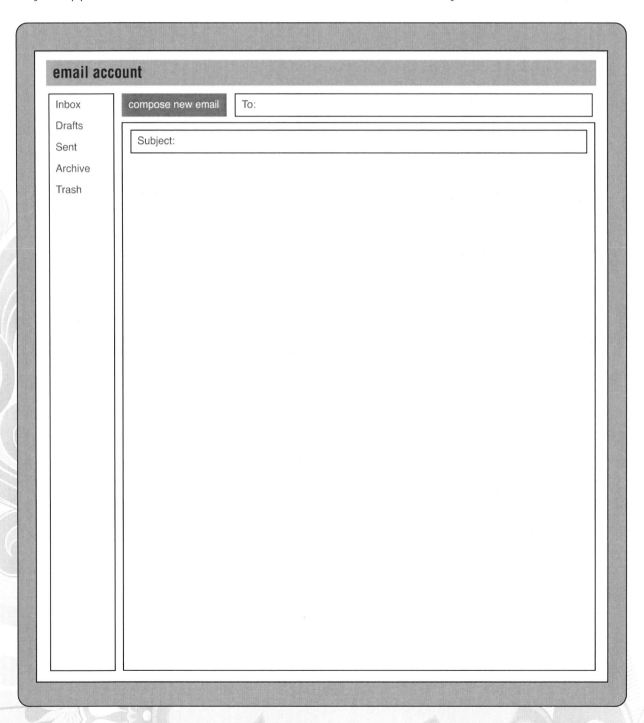

email account

Inbox

Drafts

Sent

Archive

Trash

compose new email   To:

Subject:

Not flowers again!

One of your friends has done something amazing to help you. Maybe they drove through the night to help you out, or saved your life, or helped you with a difficult project. So now you want to find an amazing way to say thank you. A bunch of flowers or a bottle of drink seems clichéd and boring. Make a list of 10 amazing or unusual ways to show your appreciation to your friend, like writing a thank you note on a helium balloon and leaving it on their doorstep. Perhaps you could try out one of your ideas and see what happens.

1
2
3
4
5
6
7
8
9
10

Grateful
Cheers
Thanks
Great
Amazing
Wow
Superb
Brilliant

Other possible thanks giving writing activities

Just for fun!
Smile file

You bring me sunshine!

Creativity
Perfect puddings

Feel-good factor
Just another perfect day

Happy maps

A few of my favourite things

The happiness experiment

Happiness pizza

Comfort blanket

Supporters' Club

Hope for the best
Rainbow of hope

Booster pack

Postcard from the future

Good news

Incredible me!
Treasured words

Best friend

And this award goes to…

To the world, with love from me

Expert witnesses

Crisis management

Objectivity

Inspired
Emergency kit

Heartfelt
The perfect love letter

31 things I like about you

Home-building

SMS

Caring hands

The kindness effect

It's the thought that counts!

Future friends

Adventures in Wonderland
Naturally amazing

Starry, starry night

Body wonderful!

Small but significant

Postcard from Wowness

Adventures in Wonderland

Wonder is experiencing something greater than ourselves, something we can't fully understand or comprehend, or someone who has achieved something of incredible beauty, power, gracefulness, sacrifice, love or complexity. We're filled with wonder when a baby is born, when we watch the massive waves of the sea bound against the rocks and smash into diamond smithereens, when we watch a man walk on the moon, or when we stop and watch a bee gather pollen from a flower.

When we're filled with wonder we may feel lost for words, because it can be difficult to describe what we have experienced. But these moments of wonder lift us up momentarily and inspire us. We may be encouraged to work harder at our own talents or studies. We may feel part of something grand and beautiful. We may feel a deeper sense of love. Our emotions have been carried above the mundane and into an experience that is thrilling and lofty.

These activities are designed to connect writers with their sense of awe. Hopefully they will experience a flavour of the positive emotions that fill their bodies when they pause and reflect on themes of wonder. It may be difficult to find all the words they need to express these intense feelings, but maybe, in the struggle, their creativity may be inspired and their aspirations may be enriched.

My hero!

Think of three people, historic or living, famous or not, who fill you with wonder, and then write why you find each of them so amazing. Write your thoughts on the plinths of their statues and sketch a suitable statue in honour of each person.

Naturally amazing

Choose one natural thing that amazes you, such as a precious stone, a bird, a mountain, a dolphin or the sea, for example. Describe it in as much detail as possible, as if you were writing to someone who had never experienced it before. Write about how it looks, sounds, feels, tastes and smells, and so on, but don't say what it really is. Then give your description to someone else and see if they can guess what you've written about.

Starry, starry night

What are some of the thoughts you have when you look at the night sky? Write each idea in a different star.

Body wonderful!

Your body is amazing! Write what you find most amazing about each of the body parts labelled below.

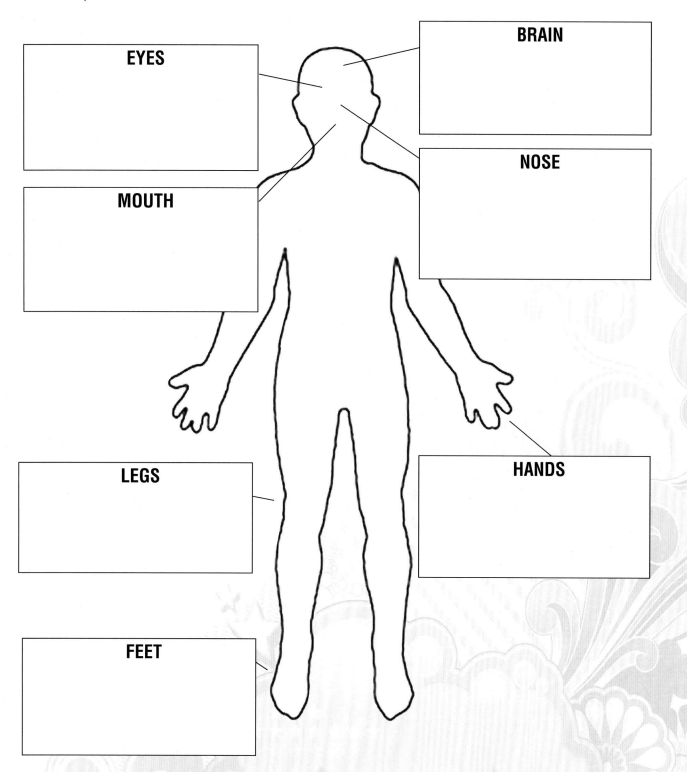

EYES

BRAIN

MOUTH

NOSE

LEGS

HANDS

FEET

Man-made wonders

You've been selected to sit on a world council that is choosing the top seven man-made wonders of the world. Each committee member has been asked to make a list of their top three wonders and to write a few lines saying why each of their 'wonders' should be included in the world's top seven. Examples might be buildings, bridges, machines, the latest computer, life-saving medical techniques, and so on.

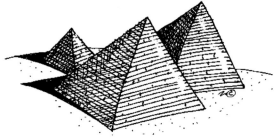

1

2

3

Small but significant

Below is a list of six natural wonders that we often take for granted because they don't stand out and grab our attention:

1. **A blade of grass**
2. **A honey bee**
3. **A cloud**

4. **A snowflake**
5. **A butterfly**
6. **A bird's egg**

Add a seventh small natural wonder of your own – something apparently ordinary, but quite amazing when you stop to think about it:

(Your small natural wonder) 7._____

On the page below rank each of the seven items in order of most wonderful (1) to least wonderful (7). Write what you find most wonderful about each of the tiny things and why you ranked it where you did.

RANK	SMALL WONDER	What I find most wonderful about this small wonder	Why I ranked this wonder where I did
1			
2			
3			
4			
5			
6			
7			

Superhero!

Imagine you've been given one incredible superpower. For example, being able to fly; being able to walk up walls; being super strong; becoming invisible; solving difficult economic or environmental problems; being able to see through walls; being able to heal people; or being a peacemaker. But you can only have the superpower for 24 hours.

Choose any superpower you like. Make up a name for yourself and write it in the title below. Then either make a careful plan for each hour of your day, or write a short story about your experience. Answer the questions in the border.

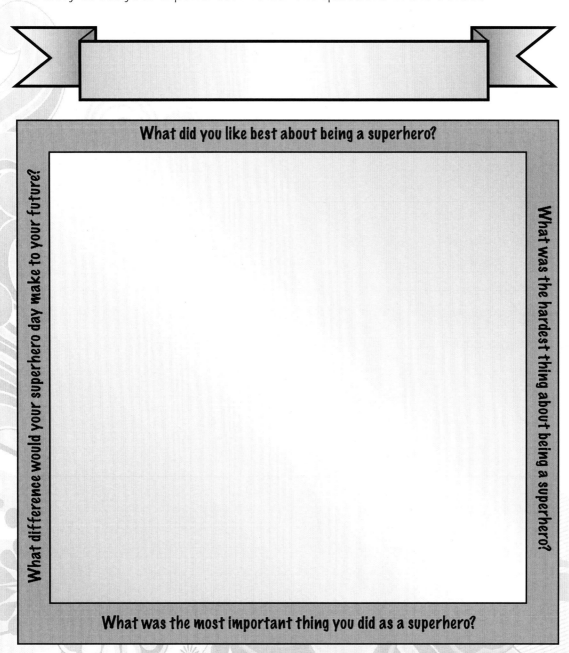

What did you like best about being a superhero?

What difference would your superhero day make to your future?

What was the hardest thing about being a superhero?

What was the most important thing you did as a superhero?

Postcard from Wowness

Think about the most amazing sight or view you have ever seen, something that just blew you away and left you speechless. Perhaps it was a snowfall; a rainbow; a brilliant sunset; the raging sea pounding the cliffs; a celebrity moment; an amazing stunt; seeing a planet through a telescope; watching an animal in the wild; or witnessing a baby taking its first steps, for example.

Below is a postcard from your moment of wonder, or Wowness. Sketch or describe the wonder on the picture side of the postcard. Then write a message describing your experience, as clearly as possible, to send to your best friend.

Art guide

Which piece of art or sculpture do you find amazing? Maybe it's a stained glass window in a cathedral; the detail of a delicate statue; an interactive art installation; a painting by Picasso; or a grand masterpiece?

Imagine that you're a tour guide telling visitors about this amazing piece of art. What would you say? Write your script below.

TOUR GUIDE BOOKLET

Wondertour!

There are many amazing places in the world: the Grand Canyon, the Great Wall of China, Niagara Falls, the Antarctic, to name a few. Imagine you are going on a superfast world tour, visiting one wonderful place a day for a week.

Write your travel plan below. You can only go around the world in a westerly direction. You must say why you'd like to go to each place, and what kind of transport you'd like to use to visit it. For example: on day 5 you might like to visit the Pyramids riding on a camel, because you've always been curious about what it was really like to be a mummy!

Day	Place	Why you want to visit it	Transport
1			
2			
3			
4			
5			
6			
7			

Other writing activities that may inpsire a sense of wonder

Hope for the best
Change the world

Save me!

Incredible me!
To the world, with love from me

Now that's interesting!
The big questions

Worthy cause

Thanks a bunch!
An alphabet of gratitude

Thanks everyone!

Glad you made it!

References

Cropley AJ (1990) 'Creativity and Mental Health in Everyday Life', *Creativity Research Journal*, 3 (3), pp167–78.

Fredrickson B (2009) Positivity: *Groundbreaking Research to Release Your Inner Optimist and Thrive*, Crown Publishing Group, New York.

Hamilton DR (2010) Why Kindness is Good for You, *Hay House UK Ltd, London.*

O'Hanlon B (2011) '25 Appreciations Before Breakfast: A Gratitude Exercise', free handout of the month, online, www.billohanlon.com (accessed July 2011).

Pettit P (2004) 'Hope and its Place in Mind', *Annals of the American Academy of Political and Social Science*, 592, pp152–65.

Provine RR (2001) *Laughter: A Scientific Investigation*, Penguin Press, New York.

Schmid T (2005) *Promoting Health Through Creativity: For Professionals in Health, Arts and Education*, John Wiley & Sons, London.

Seligman MEP (2003) *Authentic Happiness: Using the New Positive Psychology to Realize Your Potential for Lasting Fulfilment*, Nicholas Brealey Publishing, London.

Snyder CR (2002) 'Hope Theory: Rainbows in the Mind,' *Psychological Review*, 13, pp149–75.

Ueland B (1938) *If You Want to Write: A Book About Art, Independence and Spirit*, 2nd edn, Graywolf Press, St Paul.

Williams LA & DeSteno D (2008) 'Pride and Perseverance: The Motivational Role of Pride', *Journal of Personal Social Psychology*, 94 (6), pp1007–17.